Seeds of Faith for Children

Rosemarie Gortler & Donna Piscitelli
Illustrated by Mimi Sternhagen

D1466669

Our Sunday Visitor Publishing Division
Our Sunday Visitor, Inc.
Huntington, IN 46750

Nihil Obstat
Reverend Paul F. deLadurantaye, S.T.D.
Censor Deputatus

Imprimatur
✠ Most Reverend Pal S. Loverde, D.D., S.T.L., J.C.L.
Bishop of Arlington
May 29, 2012

The *Nihil Obstat* and *Imprimatur* are official declarations that a book is free from doctrinal or moral error. It is not implied that those who have granted the *Nihil Obstat* and *Imprimatur* agree with the contents, opinions, or statements expressed.

The Scripture citations used in this work are taken from the Catholic Edition of the Revised Standard Version of the Bible (RSV), copyright © 1965 and 1966 by the Division of Christian Education of the National Council of the Churches of Christ in the United States of America. Used by permission. All rights reserved.

Every reasonable effort has been made to determine copyright holders of excerpted materials and to secure permissions as needed. If any copyrighted materials have been inadvertently used in this work without proper credit being given in one form or another, please notify Our Sunday Visitor in writing so that future printings of this work may be corrected accordingly.

Our Sunday Visitor Publishing Division
Our Sunday Visitor, Inc.
200 Noll Plaza
Huntington, IN 46750
1-800-348-2440
bookpermissions@osv.com
ISBN: 978-1-61278-655-1 (Inventory No. T1350)
eISBN: 978-1-61278-290-4
LCCN: 2012955145
Cover and interior design: Amanda Falk
Cover and interior art: Mimi Sternhagen

PRINTED IN THE UNITED STATES OF AMERICA
Graphics TwoFortyFour Inc.   Wheaton, IL USA CHG45111
March 2015

This book belongs to

_____

Presented by

_____

Date

Dear Children,

This little book is all about loving and trusting God and the joy that comes from asking God to always be in our lives.

Loving and trusting God is what we call "faith."

God wants us to be really good friends with Him. Jesus told us He is our Friend, and He is with us every minute.

When we learn about our faith, we can have a closer friendship with Jesus. That doesn't mean we will never be sad or lonely. It just means that we know Jesus walks with us every single day, and He is always there to comfort us.

Trust God. Talk to Him every day, and listen when He talks in your heart. That's how faith grows from a tiny seed into a beautiful flower.

God bless you,
Rosemarie and Donna

Introduction

Being a Christian is so amazing!
When we learn about
Jesus and our faith,
it makes us want to sing —
to shout WOW —
and maybe jump up and down
with love and excitement.
Because being a Christian means
we are God's children.

It all started when God created the world.
He made all the people and the animals, too!
He sure loved us.
And He still does!
Each one of us is God's child,
no matter how old the person is.
But He especially loves little children.

God wants people to love Him and care for each other.
But a lot of people didn't believe in God.
They didn't have faith!
Because we can't see God,
it's sometimes hard to remember
that He is here,
and that He loves us.

God loves us so, so much —
        more than anyone in
            the whole wide world!
He created us,
        and we are special in His eyes.

Jesus even said
        that God knows the number
        of hairs on our head!
        He said so!

You really have to love someone a lot
        to know how many hairs are on his head —
        that's for sure!

God appreciates the little things we do
        that keep us close to Him.
When we do little things for God,
        we are telling Him,
"I love you, God, and I trust you!"

Love and trust are very, very important to God.
        Loving and trusting God
        is what our Faith is all about!

10

Did you ever plant a flower seed?
A seed needs four things to grow
into a flower.
It needs water,
air,
good dirt,
and loving care.

Guess what?
When we are baptized,
God plants a small seed of faith in us.
And you know what?
We have to take care of our seed of faith —
Like we take care of a beautiful flower.

Learning about God helps us to
know how to take care of
our seed of faith.

11

The more we learn about God,
  and pray to Him,
    and love Him,
      the more that faith seed
        will grow —

          and grow —

            and grow
            all our lives.

But what is faith?
  Faith is trusting God and
    knowing that He
      holds us in His hands!

Everything is possible with God,
  and
    someday we want to be
      with Him in heaven!

OUR·FATHER
WHO ART IN
HEAVEN·
HALLOWED
BE THY NAME
THY KINGD·M
COME · THY
WILL B DNE ON EARTH
AS IT HEAVEN · GIVE
US TH Y O DAILY·
BREAD E US
OUR T AS WE
FOR RESSPASS
AGAINS S NOT
INT DELIVER
US F MEN·

14

Prayer Helps Our Faith to Grow and Grow and Grow

It only takes a minute
        to say the prayer that
                Jesus taught the apostles.

That's **The Lord's Prayer**,
        and we call it the *Our Father*.
Jesus would love to hear you pray
        His prayer.
                Learning and praying it makes faith grow.

When we really listen to
        The Lord's Prayer,
        we hear about forgiving people.
Jesus always forgives. He taught us that
        forgiving others makes faith grow stronger.

The Lord's Prayer is a powerful way
        to help our faith grow.
Let's all be sure to REALLY join in
        loud and clear
when *The Lord's Prayer* is said by everyone
        at Mass — or any time.

God hears every little prayer we say!
He hears when we pray with our family.
God must really smile
when we get on our knees at night
to thank Him for all His gifts.

A prayer can be a long talk with God
or a simple *"Thank you, God."*
God especially loves it when we
talk to His mother, Mary.
We say the *Hail Mary* because
Mary is our mother, too!

God also gave us a special friend
to watch over us all of the time:
our guardian angel!

We can ask our guardian angel to help us
when we are sad
or hurting.
This is a prayer, too.

A quick "thank you" to God for our guardian angel
is also a wonderful prayer.

Every prayer we say grows our faith!

Our Creed – What We Believe

Did you ever notice that
      big, long prayer we say at Mass?
It's called the Creed.

The Creed is an important prayer.
      It tells us all the things we believe!
Learning this prayer helps us
      grow our faith.

This prayer says we believe in God,
      and we believe in Jesus Christ.
It also says Jesus' mother is the Blessed Virgin, Mary.

The Creed says that
      Jesus suffered so much,
            and that He died on the cross.
                People were so sad.

But then the Creed reminds us
      that on the third day,
            Jesus rose from the dead,
               and His friends
                  and mother
                     saw Him alive again!

Lots and lots of people saw Jesus alive again.
Imagine how happy they were.
Mother Mary must have cried
happy tears of joy
when she saw her Son.

The Creed tells us so much
about what we believe!
And when we read this prayer
we learn about our faith.

We can learn the words of this amazing prayer
a little bit at a time.

Praying the Creed is
a really big dose of prayer food
that makes faith grow strong!

POOL
RULES
1. NO RUNNING
2. NO BABIES BIG POOL
3. UNDER 3 MUST WEAR A LIFE VE
4. CHILDREN BE SUPERVISED
5. NO DIVING IN SHALLOW EN

3FT   3FT

The Ten Commandments
Are Rules to Grow and Grow Our Faith

Who likes rules?
>They sound so bossy.
But rules are everywhere.
We have rules at home,
>at school,
>>and in the neighborhood.
Rules are all over the place!

Even though sometimes they are no fun,
>rules help us and others to be safe.

Just think of what the world would be
>without rules — **a real mess!**
Yup! A real mess!

Cars would be crashing into each other
>without red lights.
>>Kids would probably not sleep enough
>>or eat right
>>>without Mom's rules.
We would be selfish,
>and grumpy,
>>and miserable.

23

It hurts us when someone
  lies,
    or steals,
      or gossips about us.

It hurts God, too.

Our God is so smart!
  He figured out how we could
    be healthy and happy
      and get along together.

All we have to do is follow
  His 10 rules to behave!

God's rules are called
  The Ten Commandments.
    He gave them to us
      to help us be
    the very best people we can be!

GO TO
BED on
Time! ♡
Love, Dad &
Mom

THIN ICE
STAY OFF

25

The first three commandments
tell us how to love God.

The very first rule says: Love God.

The second is: Don't use God's name
as a curse word.
And the third is: Go to Mass on Sundays
and holy days to praise God.

The other seven commandments
tell us how to love and respect
each other.

4. Obey your mom and dad.
5. Be kind. Don't hurt,
gossip about, or bully
other people.
6. We gotta respect our bodies
and other people.
7. Don't take what isn't yours.
8. Tell the truth.
9 and 10. Be happy for the gifts God gave you
and don't be jealous of others.

God knows we aren't perfect.
> But He does want us to come to heaven one day
> > to live with Him.

His rules help us know the way.
> We ask God to help us
> > do what is right.
> But if we make mistakes
> > and are sorry,
> > > we ask God to forgive us.
Asking for forgiveness is a **great big act** of trust
> that makes faith grow high as the sky!

30

The Sacraments –
Seven More Gifts to Grow Our Faith

Our Loving God!
> He thinks of everything.
When Jesus was getting ready to
> go back to His Father,
> > He wanted to be sure we would
> > > remember Him.
He gave us seven **sacraments**
> to keep us close to Him.

What are sacraments?
They are special gifts that give us the grace of God.
> Grace is like a glowing light around us
> > that helps us be holy!

The very first sacrament is **baptism.**
Most of us were baptized when we were babies.
> We don't remember it,
> > but this is when God placed
> > > the seed of faith
> > > > in our hearts.
Isn't that amazing?

Another really awesome gift
is the **Sacrament of Reconciliation.**
We call it confession.

When we go to confession, we get to
talk to a priest about our sins.
Jesus is there with the priest
even though we can't see Him.
So, we are really telling our sins to Jesus!
And Jesus forgives us.
Confession is a sacrament that helps us be
best friends with Jesus!

When we see people lining up
to go to Communion at Mass,
they are lining up for the best sacrament of all!
They are going to receive the
Body and Blood of Jesus —
even though it still looks like bread and wine.
This is the Sacrament of the **Eucharist**!
Jesus told us to do this to remember Him.

Jesus Himself changes the bread and wine
into His Body and Blood
using the priest's prayers and hands.
WOW!

"The sacraments are not magic. A sacrament can be effective only if one understands and accepts it in faith." (Youth Catechism of the Catholic Church, 177)

Jesus gave us *four* more sacraments
         to grow our faith!

Confirmation is when the Holy Spirit
         gives us gifts and graces
                  to help us live as good Catholics.
         We become like soldiers of Christ!

Matrimony is when
         a man and a woman get married
                  in the presence of Christ.

Holy Orders is when a man
         becomes a priest, or a deacon, or a bishop
                  in the Catholic Church.

The *Sacrament of the Sick*
         gives graces to people
                  when they are very sick.

Learning about the sacraments
         and receiving them
                  is how we grow our faith.
                  stronger and **stronger**!

"Sacramentals are sacred signs or
sacred actions in which a blessing is conferred."
(Youth Catechism of the Catholic Church, 272)

Holy Reminders

Sometimes we wear a holy medal
      around our necks.
It might be a crucifix, or a cross,
      or a Miraculous Medal,
         or even a saint medal.

Sometimes we keep statues
      of Jesus or Mary
         or saints in our houses.

If the medals and statues
      have been blessed by a priest,
         they are called **sacramentals**,
           which are holy reminders.

Why do we keep holy reminders?
      They're like pictures we keep
of people we love.
These pictures
      and medals
         and statues
remind us that we belong to Christ
      and that we love Him.

We talk to people we love.
　　especially God!
　　　　We say hello to God when we say:

　　　　"In the name of the Father,
　　　　and of the Son,
　　　　and of the Holy Spirit, Amen."

We say this at the beginning and end
　　of every prayer.
　　　　It's how we ask God to bless us.

We also say hello to God
　　before we eat, asking Him to bless our food.

When we bless our food and bless ourselves,
　　it's a sacramental, too!
　　　　It gets God's attention.

God loves it when we ask for His attention.

There are so many more sacramentals.
　　And when we wear them,
　　　　or hold them close,
　　　　　　or see them at church,
　　　　　　　　or talk to God,
　　　　we are making a little act of faith.

39

Faith Comes With Works

We are so lucky!
God gave us this seed of faith to grow and grow!
And He gave us everything we need
       to make our faith strong
           and to love Him.

We get to show our love of God
           every single day!

When we are kind to our neighbors —
       and Jesus told us everyone is our neighbor —
          we are loving God.

If we make a short visit to people who are sick or old,
          even if we would rather go out and play,
      that's growing our faith and loving God, too.

We can donate money or food to people in need.

Any time we do an act of charity,
       it is a work of faith
          and a prayer of love to God,
and it helps us grow and grow our faith.

Our relationship with God begins
            even before we are born.
But it doesn't end
            when we become adults.
We never want to stop learning about God.
                  He is our Friend,
                        our King,
                              and our Savior.

Prayer, especially The Lord's Prayer,
            the Ten Commandments,
                  the Creed,
                        the sacraments,
                              and works of charity
all help us grow our seed of faith
            into the most beautiful flower —
                  a relationship with God!
That's why we never stop learning about
                  our best friend,
                        Jesus, our Lord.

43

The Sign of the Cross

In the name of the Father, and of the Son,
and of the Holy Spirit, Amen.

The Lord's Prayer

Our Father, who art in heaven,
Hallowed be Thy name.
Thy kingdom come,
Thy will be done on earth, as it is in heaven.
Give us this day our daily bread,
and forgive us our trespasses,
as we forgive those who trespass against us.
Lead us not into temptation, but deliver us from evil.
Amen.

Hail Mary

Hail Mary, full of grace,
the Lord is with you.
Blessed art thou among women,
and blessed is the fruit of your womb, Jesus.
Holy Mary, Mother of God,
pray for us sinners,
now and at the hour of our death. Amen.

The Glory Be

Glory be to the Father, and to the Son, and to the Holy Spirit,
as it was in the beginning, is now, and ever shall be, world
without end, Amen.

The Apostles' Creed

I believe in God,
the Father Almighty,
Creator of heaven and earth.

and in Jesus Christ,
his only Son, our Lord.
who was conceived by
the Holy Spirit,
born of the Virgin Mary,
suffered under Pontius Pilate,
was crucified, died and was buried;
he descended into hell;
on the third day he rose again
from the dead;

he ascended into heaven,
and is seated at the right hand
of God the Father almighty;
from there he will come to judge
the living and the dead.

I believe in the Holy Spirit,
the holy catholic Church,
the communion of saints,
the forgiveness of sins,
the resurrection of the body,
and life everlasting. Amen.

Guardian Angel Prayer

Angel of God, my guardian dear, to whom God's love commits me here, ever this day be at my side, to light, to guard, to rule, to guide. Amen.

The Act of Faith

O my God, I firmly believe
that you are one God in three divine persons,
Father, Son, and Holy Spirit.
I believe that your divine Son became man
and died for our sins,
and that He will come to judge the living and the dead.
I believe these and all the truths that the holy Catholic Church teaches, because in revealing them you can neither deceive nor be deceived. Amen.

The Seven Sacraments

Baptism
Reconciliation (Confession)
First Holy Communion—and every communion we receive
Confirmation
Matrimony
Holy Orders
Sacrament of the Sick

The Ten Commandments

1. I am the Lord your God. You shall not have strange gods before me.

2. You shall not take the name of the Lord, your God, in vain.

3. Remember to keep holy the Lord's day.

4. Honor your father and your mother.

5. You shall not kill.

6. You shall not commit adultery.

7. You shall not steal.

8. You shall not bear false witness against your neighbor.

9. You shall not covet your neighbor's wife.

10. You shall not covet your neighbor's goods.

About the Authors

Rosemarie Gortler is a retired nursing instructor and continues to volunteer therapy hours as a licensed professional counselor for Catholic Charities and Project Rachel. Rosemarie is a Secular Franciscan. She and her husband, Fred, have five children, 19 grandchildren, and are now blessed with great-grandchildren.

Donna Piscitelli is a school administrator in Fairfax, Virginia. She is active in her church and in Christian outreach. She and her husband, Stephen, have four children and ten grandchildren.

Mimi Sternhagen is the mother of five grown children and is enjoying her empty nest by working for another family with five children, assisting with their homeschooling. She is a member of Regnum Christi. In addition to her collaborated work with Rosemarie and Donna, she has illustrated Catholic Cardlinks: Patron Saints and has helped with the Teach Me About series, both published by Our Sunday Visitor.